# Where Does Our Food Come From?

By Debra Stilwell

**Gareth Stevens**
Publishing

Please visit our website, www.garethstevens.com. For a free color catalog of all our high-quality books, call toll free 1-800-542-2595 or fax 1-877-542-2596.

**Library of Congress Cataloging-in-Publication Data**

Stilwell, Debra.
Where does our food come from? / Debra Stilwell.
    p. cm. — (Everyday mysteries)
Includes index.
ISBN 978-1-4339-6319-3 (pbk.)
ISBN 978-1-4339-6320-9 (6-pack)
ISBN 978-1-4339-6317-9 (library binding)
1. Agriculture—Juvenile literature. 2. Food—Juvenile literature. I. Title.
S519.S75 2012
641.3—dc23

                                2011019783


First Edition

Published in 2012 by
**Gareth Stevens Publishing**
111 East 14th Street, Suite 349
New York, NY 10003

Copyright © 2012 Gareth Stevens Publishing

Designer: Katelyn E. Reynolds
Editor: Greg Roza

Photo credits: Cover, p. 1 Stuart O'Sullivan/Stone/Getty Images; p. 5 iStockphoto.com; pp. 7, 13, 17 (fruit on truck), 19, 21, (pp. 3–24 background and graphics) Shutterstock.com; p. 9 JupiterImages/Photos.com/Thinkstock; p. 11 Jeff Rotman/The Image Bank/Getty Images; p. 15 Lester Lefkowitz/Stone/Getty Images; p. 17 David McNew/Getty Images.

Printed in the United States of America

CPSIA compliance information: Batch #CW12GS: For further information contact Gareth Stevens, New York, New York at 1-800-542-2595.

# Contents

**Boldface** words appear in the glossary.

## On the Farm

Most of the food we eat grows on farms. Fruits and vegetables are ready to eat as soon as they're picked. Other foods leave the farm and go to factories. There, the foods are used to make **processed food**.

## Crops

Many farms grow vegetables or fruits. Some grow a single kind of food, such as corn or wheat. Others grow many different crops. Farms where fruit and nut trees grow are called orchards.

apple orchard

7

# Farm Animals

Some farms raise animals for food. Livestock are animals such as cows and pigs. Birds, such as chickens and turkeys, are called poultry. Dairy farmers sell cow milk. Milk is used to make dairy **products**, such as cheese and butter.

## Seafood

Some food comes from the sea. Seafood includes fish, clams, shrimp, and even some plants. Fishing companies use large nets or traps to catch a lot of fish all at once. Some fish are raised on farms!

10

## At the Market

Some farmers sell the foods they grow at a farmers market. Markets have bins filled with fruits and vegetables. Some farmers sell milk, cheese, and other dairy products. Some even sell meats prepared on the farm.

# Food Factories

Factories use farm-grown foods to make processed foods. For example, tomatoes are used to make spaghetti sauce. **Ingredients** are added to processed food for taste or to keep it from **spoiling**. Some foods are canned or **frozen** to make them last longer.

# Shipping Food

Trucks, trains, ships, and planes carry food from farms to factories and from factories to stores. Some foods travel hundreds or thousands of miles. Some must be shipped quickly so they don't spoil. Many foods are kept frozen while they're shipped.

16

# Grocery Stores

Grocery stores sell both fresh and processed foods. Store workers take food off trucks when they arrive. Workers open boxes and place the products where they belong in the store. People from the community buy the food.

# Feed Yourself!

Some people don't shop for their food. They grow their own, just as our **ancestors** did long ago. Some people grow fruits and vegetables in gardens. Some raise chickens for eggs and meat. Others catch fish and shrimp.

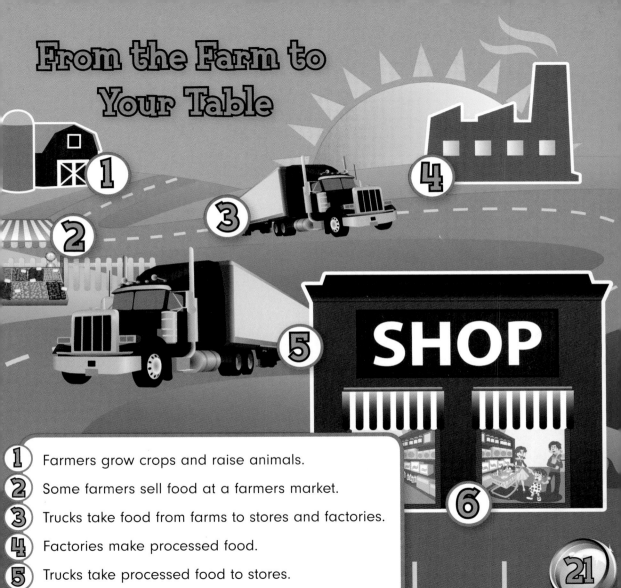

# From the Farm to Your Table

1. Farmers grow crops and raise animals.
2. Some farmers sell food at a farmers market.
3. Trucks take food from farms to stores and factories.
4. Factories make processed food.
5. Trucks take processed food to stores.
6. People in the community buy food.

SHOP

21

# Glossary

**ancestor:** someone in a family who lived long ago

**frozen:** kept very cold

**ingredient:** a food that is mixed with other foods

**processed food:** food that is changed from its original state

**product:** something made or grown that is offered for sale

**spoil:** rot

# For More Information

## Books

Adamson, Heather. *The Grocery Store*. Mankato, MN: Amicus, 2011.

Dickmann, Nancy. *Food from Farms*. Chicago, IL: Heinemann Library, 2011.

Randall, Ronne. *Where Food Comes From*. Mankato, MN: NewForest Press, 2011.

## Websites

**Fresh from the World . . . Where Your Food Comes From**
*urbanext.illinois.edu/food/*
Learn more about food and where it comes from with this colorful, animated presentation.

**FSA Kids**
*www.fsa.usda.gov/FSA/kidsapp*
Read more about how farms work on the Farm Service Agency's website.

# Index